# Brighten Your Bible Study

BY JORDAN LEE

Formatted by Katie Erickson

ISBN-13: 978-1543075700
ISBN-10: 1543075703

# TABLE OF CONTENTS

# Introduction

Hey girl (or boy, boys are welcome, too). If you're here, it's probably because you want to enhance your bible study. Awesome. Let's do it. But before we get started, I have two things for you.

A tip:
You will only get out of this what you put in. I'm going to reveal to you all the little ways my personal bible study has been enhanced with splashes of creativity and connectivity. I'll unveil the things I've tried and chosen not to stick with as well as the things I've liked and chosen to stick with. I'm sharing both because, well, you're a different human with a different soul than me and you might just like what I didn't. You like chocolate. I like vanilla, whatever. As long as we both like Jesus, it's all-good.

A story:
I want to tell you what a stinky pair of shoes taught me about studying the Bible. Last summer, I started wearing my white tennis shoes without socks because I didn't have those tiny little socks that are nearly invisible and pairing my hot pink and neon yellow socks looked awfully funny. I have obnoxious socks because I don't believe in boring. Who needs normal? We've got enough of that.
Anyway, I chose to forgo sock wearing with my white shoes because I wanted to at least try to look like I had a clue about fashion. As a result of walking around with sweaty feet and no socks, my shoes got pretty stinky. They looked lovely but smelled awful. I washed them once but the material shrunk in the dryer and my poor little feet were squeezed to death the first few days of wearing them again. So at that point, it was either throw out the white shoes, wear them stinky, or sport the neon socks proudly. I chose the latter. I couldn't part with

the shoes. But they were stinky without socks so I spiced them up with the hot pink ones.

I know, I know. You're probably thinking, "Why didn't she just buy new socks?" That would have been far too logical. But it's a good thing that I didn't run and buy new socks because my stinky shoe experience inspired a much deeper and more enriching experience when it came to studying Scripture.

Here's why: Think of my stinky white shoes like the pages of the bible. Just like the shoes complete every outfit, the Word points to what completes every soul on this planet: God alone. But appreciating the shoes is hard when they are stinky. We may stop wearing them completely. In the same way, appreciating the Word is hard when our study is stinky, boring, and bland. We may stop reading it completely, only because we don't have the proper tools to get rid of the stink.

We can wash our shoes, which temporarily fixes the stink problem but they may hurt our feet, and eventually, if we keep wearing them as we did before, they will begin to stink again. In the same way, we can come the Word with a new approach, try a wicked new bible study with lovely little devotions each day but if we're just checking Bible Study of the to-do list, making it look neat and pretty, we're going to have a hard time experiencing Jesus abundantly. And eventually, our Bible study will be boring, bland, and stinky again. Just like the stinky white shoes.

So what's my point? When I stopped worrying about doing "normal", when I took a risk and let my neon socks show, my shoes weren't stinky and I actually wanted to wear them. I'd like to say that my fun socks made wearing my shoes more fun, more vibrant, and livelier. The same goes for my bible study. When I began to unpack the Word instead of just skimming it or strictly following a neat and tidy study plan, I chose to make it a vibrant, personal, and lively experience. I was tired of a stinky bible study.

Everyone was raving about the bible, so I set out to find ways to make it come to life in my personal life. I shook off the lies that told me how I should study the Word and met God in prayer. Some argue that it's wrong to mark up my Bible; some say it's destructive and disrespectful. But you know what? The fashion police probably would say the same thing about pairing neon socks with cute white shoes, but it worked for me.

So from that point on, I decided to get creative and really experience intimacy and freedom when learning His Word. And I want you to experience this same freedom.

Can I take your hand and whisper a Truth that I wish someone had told me?

Let yourself interact with the Word. God gave you His Word so that you may know Him, His heart, His character, and His plan. It's not disrespectful to let your walk with Him be vibrant. Let your time studying Scripture become vibrant, colorful, and alive. God isn't dead. He isn't the fashion police. He's a friend and a Father. Get to know Him. And *enjoy* getting to know Him. Enjoy wearing the Word in your heart. Let it be splashed full of neon colors and notes and every other mark that brings it to life for you.

I'm a firm believer that *when we learn to be messy before God, in His Word and at His feet, we become equipped to be bolder for Him in this big world.*

As you try applying these methods to your bible study, give yourself permission to add your own mojo. It shouldn't look just like mine or like your sisters'.

Use these ideas as a guideline, a starting point, and then go. Go crazy in getting to know God. And if you need a boatload of highlighters to do it, then get a boatload of high lighters. Don't be ashamed of a vibrant relationship with Jesus. You will be better for it.

# I Like Big Bibles

I love taking notes. Maybe you do, maybe you don't. But notes are a crucial part of digging in the Word because they help you retain what you learn. Think about it. If you're going to study physics, you're not going to retain much without writing out the problems, the important formulas, and whatever else smart science-y people do. I wasn't a science-y person. I threw up when I dissected a frog in fifth grade, so my biology career ended early. But you get my point. If you want to learn Scripture, write the notes, scribble the sticky statements you want to remember, and spill your soul across the page. Because you when you do, they will stick in your brain and be written across your heart deeper than if you only skim the text.

Taking notes in a journal is fantastic. Go for it. It's great for reference. I use a journal and I love it. But I realized that having my notes about a certain passage right where that passage is makes such a difference. If I happen to study that passage months later, the notes from what I learned before are right there to reference and I don't have to go digging through my eighteen million journals to find contextual and personal notes. It's right there, on the page.

It's hard to take notes on tiny bible pages. You need room. You need space to create, write, and curate. I suggest getting a big journaling bible. I use the **ESV Single Column Journaling Bible by Crossway Books.**

In addition to Crossway, there are several other places you can find a journaling bible, such as Amazon or Lifeway.

# The Tool Bench

I'm pretty sure my readers think I use all sorts of fancy tools to study the Bible. The pages messy and splashed full of colorful and notes. I love it. I left it in an airport bathroom once. I know that sounds weird. I wasn't bible studying and bathroom-ing simultaneously.

I carried it with me when I got off the plane, and set it down on the sink counter. Thankfully, I realized that it was missing and sprinted through the crowd back to the restroom and found it right where I had left it. There has been so much swirling, twirling, curating, and cultivating in those pages that I may have passed out if I lost it.

So, in case you were wondering, all is good now. My bible is safe and sound tucked into the corner of my bookshelf.

Okay, back to tools. I'm going to be very clear about this because I think it tends to become very confused and overthought inside the world of bible journaling and: YOU. DO. NOT. NEED. FANCY. TOOLS.

Please, please, please, please, please (did I say please?) do NOT spend half, or even a quarter, of your paycheck at a craft store buying all sorts of fancy tools because then it becomes more about your creation than the Creator. And that's backwards so let's just not even go there.

Get yourself a pack of basic sharpie highlighters, either at Wal-Mart or in your junk drawer. These have minimal bleed through and they get the job done just fine. And scrounge up a regular, household pen. I think I've been using one that I found in a hotel room or something. People, the point is not to have pretty pens. The point is to write purposefully on the page. A pretty pen and a boring pen can both accomplish that.

And that's it
for tools.
Seriously.
You don't
need to get
fancy kits or
anything
even close to
it. Your
bible is a
living,

breathing story and love letter. (Technically, the phrase says that it's a "living, breathing document." And that's true but it's also a story of God's love and plan for all of us.

These study methods will help you dissect it and enjoy its vibrancy but it won't turn it into a scrapbook. A few simple highlighters will do the trick.

I also mark the chapters with washi tape. You can find it at any craft store and I'm pretty certain that the roll I bought was 99 cents. So that's basically the cost of a small french fry from McDonald's, but if you can sacrifice the fries, I promise it's totally worth it.

Like I said, my bible is not a scrapbook. Although the tape makes it look pretty, which is always nice, it serves a purpose in my Bible. I use it to mark the beginning of every book of the Bible.

So for example, the first page of Genesis has tape with a polka dot pattern folded over the edge, the first page of Exodus has tape with a stripe pattern folded over the edge,

Leviticus has a solid blue piece of tape folded over the edge, and so forth. It simply helps me find each book when I crack open the Bible.

# WHERE TO START

There's a really great book called *Women of the Word* by Jen Wilkin. She's fantastic. This book helps answer the big question, "Where should I even begin and how do I read the Bible? Do I just open to whatever page and hope God speaks to me through what I find? Do I read through it chronologically? What's a girl to do?"

Jen addresses these questions and more with very detailed and insightful answers. I would love to go through every tidbit of wisdom she shares, but this guide would end up being 190 pages long. So to get a better understanding of how to read the Bible, I suggest that you grab her book.

However, I will offer a few starting points that have helped me. I've tried several ineffective ways to study, such as what Jen calls the *Magic Eight Ball* approach. In this approach, the reader simply opens the Bible to a random page and hopes to be touched by something. Long story short, don't do this. It will leave you disappointed because if you really want to learn something and digest it, it will need to be more than an emotional or feel-good experience. Although it is spiritual, and although you will inevitably have many emotional and personal experiences during your time in the Word (as you should!) you will also have times where you just don't *feel* it. If you are studying with the *Magic Eight Ball* approach and feel like you didn't "get anything out of it", you may find yourself discouraged. Plus, you won't be able to see how it all works together and may have a hard time understanding what it's really saying.

Just like you can't learn algebra by flipping a math textbook to page 120 and hoping it speaks to you, you can't learn the rich lessons in the Bible properly with this style of studying.

And just like you don't expect to have some incredible emotional experience or even to understand it when studying algebra for the first time, you don't need to expect that you'll fully comprehend or even really feel good about everything you digest when you first dive into the Word. But if you put in personal time, patience, intentionality, and purpose, instead of relying on emotions or the chance of coming across a feel-good passage, you will have an enriched experience over time.

Before I give you a suggestion on where to start, I want to give you a little overview of what the Bible is ultimately about. I'll try to keep this to just a few lines.

Essentially, the Bible is a story *about* God. It's one big story that ties itself together in a neat little bow with a grace-filled ribbon weaving through and unites the books, stories, passages, prophecy, and poetry—ultimately pointing to God's plan of redemption.

The Bible is God's story of redemption, His ultimate rescue mission, that reveals the desperate need we have for Him and His deep desire to reunite us to Himself.

In regards to the "where to start" question, there's really no wrong answer. Personally, I suggest starting with the gospels. Some people would suggest starting in Genesis and reading the Bible from start to finish but I loved starting in the gospels. This helped me refresh my understanding of the core of Christianity and then I was able to see how all other writings and stories point in some way to the ultimate resolution of Christ's life, death, and resurrection.

There are four gospel books: Matthew, Mark, Luke and John. These are all eyewitness accounts of Jesus' life on earth as told by those He spent time with on earth. You will notice a lot of repetition and connectivity between these four books but you will also notice ways that they fulfill many prophecies and even law from the Old Testament.

Additionally, different parts of different stories are included in some accounts and not included in others. This helps paint a fuller picture for you as a reader and gives us even more reason to believe they are true, factual accounts. Think about it. If four different people go to an event, each one will experience it slightly differently. They will each notice different things. Just because four people participate in the same activity doesn't mean they will all see it exactly the same. The same goes for the gospel writers. Matthew noticed something Mark may not have and vice versa.

If you draw those connections and take note of the ways everything works together in these accounts, it will surely enrich your understanding and experience. However, wherever you begin studying, always consider context. Take note of the audience—to whom these book were being written, ask WHO wrote it, and ask WHEN & WHY they were being written (Google it if you don't know). Jot this down because context is key.

Something else I like to do is pick a book of the Bible and read through it entirely, a little bit each day. Use the methods laid out in this guide to study it and you'll see find that not only are you reading just that book of the Bible, but pieces of several other books, because of how interconnected and unified Scripture really is. For example, you may be reading a chapter in the book of 1 Peter 2, but as you study and apply these study methods, you may be hopping over to Isaiah 28:16, Psalm 118:22, and Isaiah 8:14 to see what Peter may be referencing from the Old Testament.

## Taking Notes: Ask Questions

The Bible is a big book with lots of words. Dissecting them, understanding them, and then writing down everything we learn from them can be overwhelming and also slightly confusing. Let's un-confuse (not a word, whatever) our brains by breaking down what we *should* be pulling out of Scripture and why.

First things first. The Bible isn't made to an instruction manual or a book about us and what we should do. Although it gives us a ton of guidance for following Christ, we can't read it as a handbook to life. The Bible is a book about God. It reveals His story and plan *for* His people. It reveals His nature, purpose, and character in every passage. We can literally learn something about God in all parts of the bible, from law to prophecy to poetry.

A helpful question to ask as you read is, "What is this passage teaching me about God, His character, or His purpose? And by looking at who God is, what does this teach me about who I am as His daughter?"

There may be several answers to this within a passage. Actually, there almost always is. Take note of this. Circle a phrase within the passage that teaches you something about God, His plan, etc. Then draw a little arrow to the margins. Write what you learned in the margins and draw a box around it so that it doesn't get mixed up with all the other notes you're about to learn how to take.

One of the best ways to take notes is to ask questions as we read and then to take note of the answers. This helps us see the unity within the Word, gain insight into how a passage relates to the big story that the Bible is telling, and uncover its relevance to our life.

Here are a few examples of the questions to ask:
1. What is the main plot, argument, or idea in this passage?
2. What character flaws, sin, or difficulties are presented?
3. How does the narrative or passage begin to point to Christ's ultimate resolution?
4. How is God calling me to respond?

# TAKING NOTES: Discover the Main Idea

When I study, I love pull the main idea out of a passage and write it across the top of the page. This helps me both visualize and remember the message that really stands out as I read. I typically use bold block or script letters so that I don't miss it if I ever happen to skim that same passage again in the future.

For example, I recently studied in Zechariah 1-3. Chapter 3 gives a really neat vision that the prophet, Zechariah, has. Many commentaries and interpretations of this vision believe this to be a Messianic vision, a foreshadowing of Christ.

The vision illustrates a courtroom scene. I'll set it up for you. In this passage, Joshua represents people (aka the world) standing before the angel of the Lord. Satan is standing as the accuser, God is the judge, and Jesus serves as Joshua's (the defendant) defense attorney—or, advocate.

The word "Messiah" is the Hebrew word for "advocate." Jesus, in His perfect righteousness, stands in our place and God drops all the charges and we are reconciled to the offended person, or in this case, God our Father. How beautiful is that?

So to remember this big concept, I would write, "Christ our Advocate" across the top of the page.

This is certainly something I don't want to forget!

# TAKING NOTES: Supplemental Resources

I also suggest taking notes about contextual clues to help you understand the words. I use LOGOS+ Bible App as well as some other commentaries to do this. I'm not a walking encyclopedia and I'm sure you're not either. Don't be afraid to use resources that help provide the contextual information that can be key to understanding a passage on a deeper level.

For example, in Ephesians 2:5, there is a phrase that says we are "made alive together with Christ." The Greek translation of the word "together" is "syzōopoeiō". In Greek, this word conveys action. So if you use your supplemental resources, you might learn that this part of the passage is essentially saying that Christ, the head, is being seated at God's right hand and the body (the church, you and me) also sits there with Christ.

This context clue shows that we are already seated IN Him (Christ) and that we will be seated BY Him. We are in Him—our identity, purpose, and entire being is seated in Him. This is the ground of our hope. After this life, when He will seat us at His right hand and hope will no longer be necessary because we will literally be at His right hand, together with Christ.

What insight! We could have flown right past that simple phrase but taking the time to unpack the meaning is incredibly eye opening to understand the original text.

Take notes of this and draw a little box around the translations and meanings as well.

I also take notes by writing down what I learn in a devotional or a book that I'm reading. Solid, Truth-centered books (do your research!) can serve as a wonderful supplemental resource to understanding the text. For example, when I read *The Meaning of Marriage* by Tim Keller. Utilizing his teaching alongside my study of the verses that he referenced helped me understand the Scripture on a deeper level.

It also helped me find ways to practically apply the Truth to marriage. For example, as he pulled out important concepts from Ephesians 5, I wrote down the most important points in the right hand column. This wasn't a formal devotional study but it was guidance that helped me as I focused my heart on what Truth says about marriage. Make sense?

When I write down an important lesson from Scripture right next to the passage itself, I tend to remember what I studied much more. It sticks when I write. The same is true for many people.

Don't be afraid to write and rewrite. Write until there's no room left on the page. Write the lesson you learned from a resource, the contextual clues, paralleling verses, your questions (and answers!), personal reflections, and more. Actually, this is a smart study tip for anything you're studying, whether it is the Bible, a math lesson, or a training manual from work. Supplemental resources, whether it is commentaries or books, can and will enrich your study because they help unpack the words on the page when our eyes would otherwise glaze over. Just do your homework and make sure you check your source—if it doesn't line up with Truth or seems to preach the prosperity gospel, be cautious and consult a trusted Biblical mentor.

# TAKING NOTES: Discover Connections

The Bible is incredibly unified. There are connections everywhere – within passages, within books, and between different passages in different books! There are several core concepts and ideas repeated over and over in a variety of contexts throughout the whole Bible.

There is an amazing grace-filled strand that weaves every Word and Truth noted in the text of Scripture together in a way unexplainable by the human mind. Remember that the books of the Bible were all written at different times, by different authors divinely inspired by God, which leaves only a supernatural explanation for the unity and consistency that it maintains. It only further proves that the divine heart of an all-knowing God has penned every word of Scripture.

Anyway, finding these connections and visualizing them by drawing connectors and taking notes will open your eyes to a whole new world (cue Aladdin theme music). Really, though, it's incredible!

Let me give you an example of connections to draw within a book of the Bible. If you flip to 2 Corinthians 6-7, you'll see a repeated idea: *widen your heart* and *make space* for God. It is said in 2 Corinthians 6:11 and then said again in 2 Corinthians 7:2. Then, the repetition points to something in 2 Corinthians 7:4, "I am overflowing with joy." So write down what the connections within this passage teach us: *Widen your hearts and let God in because a life that is open to interruption from God is joyful because joy comes from God.*

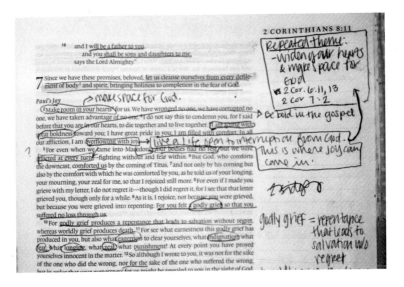

I typically circle the places where an idea or phrase is repeated and then draw a line between each circle to connect the repeated idea. It makes the repetition visual and tangible and it helps the reader discover the message God is trying to teach her. If you see something several times, chances are, God is speaking into you–He wants you to get it. Take note!

Next, we want to see if any part of a passage is prophesized or discussed at other places in the Good Book. The Author and Perfecter of our faith divinely inspired the Bible and therefore it is consistent and unified throughout the books, chapters, and Testaments. Chances are, with a little digging, you will find other places in Scripture that the concept you are studying is repeated.

I'll give you an example of connections between books in the Old and New Testaments. One way to find it is to simply pay attention to the text. If you were reading in 2 Corinthians 6:14-18, you would come upon verse 16 which says, "For we are the temple of the living God; *as God said…*"

CONNECTION ALERT!

God said this somewhere before. Find the verses that are being referenced by checking out the coordinating footnotes at the bottom of the page. Usually there's a little annotation within the passage. If you don't find it there, try using a commentary. With a little effort, you will find that **Leviticus 26:12** and **Isaiah 53:11** are being referenced in 2 Corinthians 6:16-18. WRITE IT DOWN!

I jot down the two verses referenced right next to the passage I'm studying. See image.

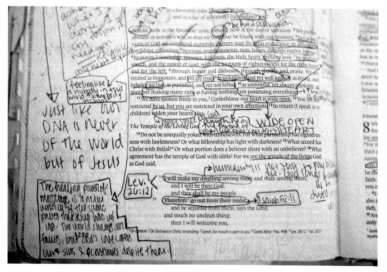

Then, I flip to the referenced passage(s) and make a small note to "see 2 Corinthians 6:16-18." In this case, I would jot this down next to Leviticus 26:12 and Isaiah 53:11. When I come across these passages again in the future, I will be reminded of the connections and remember what I learned the first time.

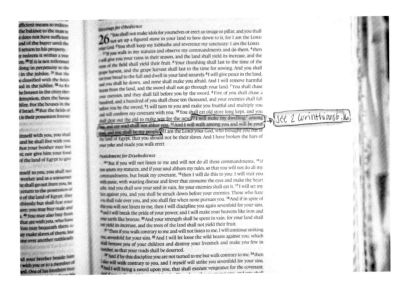

As mentioned before, supplemental study tools can make a big difference. Don't be afraid to use devotionals or books or commentaries to help draw connections.

For example, when I read *God's At War* by Kyle Idleman, I simply studied the Scriptures referenced in each chapter as I read his book. This served as a topical study about the idols (relationships, work, etc.) that fight for our hearts and attention in our daily life.

On the subject of love and relationships, it referenced a passage in 1 Corinthians 7:17-39 and connected it to concepts outlined in Galatians 5:13, 1 Peter 2:16 and in Matthew 11:29-30. The overarching theme that connected these four passages?

*LOVE makes service in Christ perfect freedom.*

Our freedom from idols and bondage comes from bowing to and serving the God who loves us over bowing to and serving gods in our life—idols that don't love us but to rule and enslave us. Keeping this in mind, I was able to draw connections between all of the referenced passages and take notes in the margins of those verses as the book discussed each one. I also wrote the overarching theme across the top of the page. See image example.

Whenever you see something like this during a topical study or through a book you're reading, don't skim over it. It's so much more powerful when we take a moment to crack open the Bible and take note of it. As you discover connections, be sure to write down verses that parallel each other or a specific passage you are studying in the margins and draw a box around it to keep it organized. Your page will come to life!

## HIGHLIGHTING: Organize

I began using highlighting in an attempt to organize the insane amount of notes that I cram onto a page. Now that you've read about my note taking methods, I want to focus on the purpose of this highlighting method as well as share why it's helpful. This is my method of choice because it adds a touch of color and creativity to the pages

without taking away the most important part: the message. When you take notes in a journaling bible, you have a lot of blank space to write in the margins. If you're anything like me, your natural handwriting is significantly larger than the tiny little text on the page. So, I often write a note off to the side in the margin. For example, if I'm studying a passage and I want to write a note about verse 6 in the blank space, chances are that my note will run further down the page than where verse 6 ends. Or, I will have several notes from other verses or words cluttering the page and will need a way to differentiate what verse or word each note is referring to.

Here's how I keep it organized: I highlight the verse I'm referring to and then draw an arrow to the note about that verse (likely in the margins). Then, I highlight the arrow AND draw a box around the note in the same color that I highlighted that verse with. If I happened to take a note on another verse later, I would do the same thing with a different color highlighter to differentiate between the notes. It adds a splash of color to your pages while keeping with intentionality. The photo below is a simple example.

## HIGHLIGHTING: Color Code

Another highlighting method that I want to share with you is what I call "color-coding."
I use this method to help visualize the repeated themes and context of passages.

I honestly have a love-hate relationship with it. I love it because it does help with dissecting the passage and helping the reader understand context within the verses. It also helps focus and basically forces me to read each word very closely. However, it can be incredibly tedious, especially with a longer study. I would recommend using this method for shorter studies and smaller passages. And don't feel pressured to highlight every single word that falls into each color category. I tried that and it almost defeats the purpose. The point is to highlight intentionally and bring out the most impactful words, phrases, and themes. The best time to use the color-coding system is when you notice a lot of repetition or if you find something complex that you want to break down in order to get a better understanding of it.

Below you'll find the color-coding system that I've used (but feel free to create your own!):

Green: Main Idea
Purple: Repeated theme, idea, or imagery
Pink: Key transitions (ie. "Therefore", always ask what it's there for)
Yellow: Strong verbs and action words
Blue: Powerful descriptors/descriptions of God (i.e. "Living water")
Orange: Problems and/or descriptions of people (i.e. "Broken")

# HIGHLIGHTING: Break It Down

Another method that I've found helpful is a verse-by-verse high light. This pairs with a specific note taking method as well. Hand in hand, the two really help dissect whichever passage you may be studying. I do this so that I can pull apart each verse, piece by piece, or in this case, word by word.

Here's how it works:
First, I highlight an entire verse with a specific color in order to differentiate it from surrounding verses.

Next, I either underline or circle any words that initially stand out to me. Then, I use the LOGOS+ Bible app on my phone, search said verse, and source not only commentaries but also translations of the words that I found stood out to me. I often like to find the Hebrew or Greek context for many of the words, which almost always gives me a whole new level of understanding of the context and purpose behind the word and phrases.

FYI: The Old Testament was written in Hebrew and the New Testament was written in Greek and Aramaic.

Let's say I find the appropriate Greek translation or context for the word "together" in a certain passage using a commentary or the LOGOS+ Bible app.

I would circle the word together, draw a little arrow, and then write the note with the translation and any other contextual information that would be helpful to understanding the whole verse or passage.

Additionally, I would also take a note of any connections made within other books of the Bible. Highlighting these connections in the same color is incredibly valuable to understanding the Good Book as a WHOLE. Highlight this passage, write a note about the verse in the Old Testament it points to so that you don't forget later on, and then TURN to the actual verse in the Old Testament that it is referencing. Highlight that verse in the same color and write in the New Testament verse that relates to it. Refer to pages 17-18 for photo examples of this note taking + highlight method used together

The LOGOS+ app, as well as other commentaries, will help you find beautiful nuggets of Truth nestled within the connections and context of a passage. When you begin intentionally drawing connections between books and between the Old and New Testaments, I promise you this: you will be amazed at how interconnected and unified the Bible is. You'll probably want to highlight the heck out of it! So do it. No one is stopping you.

The words and pages and stories are woven together so undeniably beautifully and the more you see that, the more you'll *want* to dive into the Word. It will enrich

your understanding of God and His Word, as well as your Bible study experience. Look for connections and for context as you break down each verse and watch the Word become more than just informative – it will become transformative!

# THE BOTTOM LINE: There Are No Rules

Now that you have some ideas, burn this guide. Really, I won't be offended. Here's why: I don't want you to be come a robot Bible studier. Don't be so worried about exact methods and study tips that you lose the study itself. Enjoy it. Make it personal. Modify the methods provided in this guide to fit your needs. Combine them. Actually, many of these work together as one – breaking each one down into it's own individual study method has been difficult because they go together so well.

Pick the ones you like, pitch the ones you don't. Let the Spirit guide your study, open your mind to trying new things, splatter some color on the pages, and spill your soul as you do. Your notes can be something as simple as a personal reflection, a prayer, or whatever else God lays on your heart. At the end of the day, your time in the Word is between you and God. It can be as messy and unorganized as it needs to be as long as you're letting the message sink in. There are several pages of my Bible I don't share photos of. Some I feel compelled to share but many are my dialogue between God and me alone. Give yourself this freedom, too.

***There are no rules for getting to know God.*** Get alone with Him and let Him pour love into your heart. Then spill it out, across the pages of the Word and across places of the world. You won't just encounter Him by having a more beautiful Bible study. Don't stop there. Let what you learn propel you out of your comfy corner and get out into the world. Meet His people. Feed them. Clothe them. Love them. Pray with them. Be bold in your witness and you'll experience not only a brighter Bible study, but also a brighter life. Because like I always say, messy in the WORD = confident in the WORLD.

**For more, follow online:**

WEBSITE: www.thesoulcripts.com
FACEBOOK: www.Facebook.com/soulscripts
INSTAGRAM: instagram.com/soulscripts
TWITTER: twitter.com